OM at Home

Written and Illustrated
by Cyndi Lee

CHRONICLE BOOKS

SAN FRANCISCO

ISBN 0-8118-3888-9

Designed by Laurie Dolphin
Illustrations by Cyndi Lee
Manufactured in China

Distributed in Canada by
Raincoast Books
9050 Shaughnessy Street
Vancouver, B.C. V6P 6E5

10 9 8 7 6 5 4 3 2 1

Chronicle Books LLC
85 Second Street
San Francisco, CA 94105
www.chroniclebooks.com

Not all exercises are suitable for everyone. Your physical condition and health are important factors in determining which yoga exercises, positions, and advice may be appropriate. This or any other exercise program may result in injury. The author and publisher of this book disclaim any liability from any injury that may result from the use, proper or improper, of any exercise or advice contained in this book. Please consult your professional health care provider for information and advice on the suitability of your exercise program.

OM at Home

A Yoga Journal

my yoga journal

Keeping a journal is a time-honored method of reflecting on our lives, of noticing what goes on both outside of our bodies and inside our hearts. Recording your private journey through the natural rhythms of life gives you a way to make sense of your experiences and to let that knowledge deepen your understanding of yourself. In fact, this journal may inspire you to learn more about what is already there inside you, waiting to be discovered through contemplation and writing.

Practicing yoga is another way to become more familiar with yourself. It is also a method for cultivating a variety of skillful means—patience, generosity, compassion, discipline—that can help you lead a more balanced, harmonious, and healthy life. When done mindfully, yoga can become a powerful path to waking up to the vibrancy of your everyday life. There is really nothing more compelling than experiencing your own life at the same time as you are living it.

This journal is divided into four sections that correspond to the four seasons of the natural year. As each season arises we are newly awakened to the changes in our environment and how those changes affect our physical and mental energy. Often a swirl of spontaneous memories floats up to the surface of our consciousness, reminding us of the continuity of life, the familiarity of seasonal rituals, and the recognition of, or surprise at, our responses from year to year.

how to use this journal

The four yoga programs in this journal are designed to match the natural energy of their corresponding season: blooming spring, outgoing summer, mellow autumn, and quiet winter. Every season's program contains thirteen *asanas*, or poses, that correspond to each week in the season. I recommend doing the entire thirteen-pose sequence daily, but you can also focus on the pose of the week or create your own short sequences, based on your schedule and physical stamina.

Try to begin each day's yoga practice with the daily warm-up, which will prepare you for each season's longer program. Since each season logically unfolds into the next, as you go through the year, you can choose to keep adding on. For example, in the spring you will do the daily warm-up and then the sun salute. In the summer you will do the daily warm-up, sun salute, and then standing poses and hip openers. By the end of the year you will have gained the ability to do a full program, which includes all the basic elements of yoga. Make a commitment to end each practice with the daily relaxation.

The sequence of seasonal yoga programs is designed to warm up your body, develop strength, energize, and then relax. Although the journal begins in spring, you can maintain this sequence even if you begin using it in the summer, autumn, or winter. You will still begin your practice with the daily warm-up, then do the program for the current season, but as the year unfolds, change the order of your practice so it begins to match the journal sequence. For example, if you begin with winter, when spring arrives, change the order so spring is first in your practice.

Then when summertime comes, do spring, summer, winter. Then spring, summer, autumn, and winter. If you begin with autumn, do autumn, winter, and then spring, autumn, winter. Then spring, summer, autumn, and winter. Always end with winter.

The questions that appear on each week's pages are designed to help you integrate your yoga *asana* experience with your daily life. You can think about these questions anytime: before, during, or after your practice, and you can write about them in the space provided. You can also use the space to write anything else about your yoga practice that you want to remember.

daily warm-up

This sequence is designed to loosen up your entire spine, including your neck, which in turn will energize your entire body. It will also open your hip and shoulder joints, your wrists and ankles, and your elbows and knees and get you ready for the rest of the practice for each season.

daily relaxation

At the end of every yoga class we rest by lying on our backs, with eyes closed. This is called corpse pose. In this pose we let go of all physical effort, including any special breathing techniques, and simply relax. After five to ten minutes, begin to deepen your breathing again. Roll onto your right side and rest there for a moment. Then, slowly, letting your head be the very last thing to come up, use your hands to walk your body back up to sitting.

general yoga tips

Try to move in harmony with your breath.

Notice the transitions between poses as much as you notice the poses themselves.

See everything along the way. Look up right now and see what is in front of you. Feel free to stay in any one pose for a while and explore it with your breath.

Try to stay in each pose for at least five breaths; one inhale and one exhale equals one breath. Work up to ten breaths in each pose, unless otherwise indicated.

breathing and mindfulness

In yoga we breathe both in and out through the nose. As you breathe deeply, use the movement of the breath as a resting place for your mind. Watch the path of your breath and see where it goes easily and where it gets stuck. Don't worry about it; just begin to learn about your breathing patterns. Watch how they change. When you realize that you have gotten caught up in thinking, gently return your attention to your breath. If you can apply this level of mindfulness to your yoga practice, you will begin to balance your inner and outer awareness, and experience an awakening. That awakening is food for your journal.

inhale $\longrightarrow$ 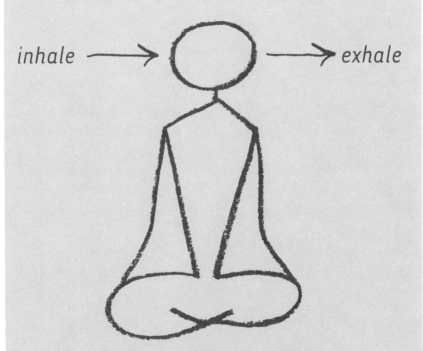 $\longrightarrow$ exhale

Sit in the easy-pose position.

Daily Warm-Up

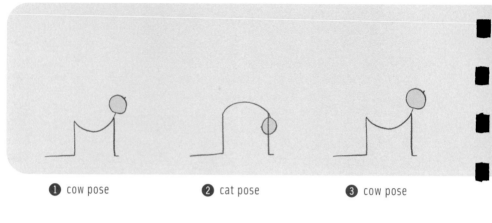

1 cow pose   **2** cat pose   **3** cow pose

7 hands and knees   **8** threading the needle to the left   **9** child's pose

13 shoulder stretch   **14** side bend to the left

4 downward dog

5 hands and knees

6 threading the needle to the right

10 roll up to sitting

11 arm circle

12 chest opener

15 shoulder stretch

16 side bend to the right

Spring: *FINDING OUR PLACE IN THE SUN*
The Sun Salute

After the long cold months of winter, who doesn't start to long for the sun? The warmth in our bones, the heat on our skin, the light on our face—they're like food for the heart. We all recognize that energy lift we get from the unfolding of spring. Many cultures have rebirth myths that correspond with the springtime, the lengthening of days, the renewal of life, the possibility of a fresh start.

By practicing the sun salute we too can feel this primal connection. The sun salute is an invitation to experience our universal connection to the life force of the sun, this ocean of heat energy that we all swim in together. It invites us to relax the tight grip we have on our immediate concerns and gain some perspective on our place in the big picture. What a relief!

The *vinyasa* form of yoga, matching breath and movement, creates heat in our bodies, which opens our joints, flushes out toxins, and makes our muscles more pliable. The most essential form of *vinyasa* is the sun salute, which, when done mindfully, can be a vigorous, uplifting, and spacious way to begin the day.

When the weather has been cold or rainy for longer than we like, sometimes we joke at OM Yoga Center that we need to do more sun salutes. And, in the springtime, anyway, it does feel as if the sun hears us and responds by staying out a little bit longer every day.

Spring

4 lunge, right leg back

5 downward dog

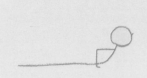

8 baby cobra

9 downward dog

12 mountain pose with arms overhead

13 mountain pose

Spring: THE SUN SALUTE

1 mountain pose

2 mountain pose with arms overhead

3 standing forward bend

6 plank pose

7 knees, chest, chin

10 lunge, right leg forward

11 standing forward bend

The Sun Salute

Try to do at least four sun salutes—two to each side—but feel free to do more. Take as long as you like, but it probably won't take you longer than five to ten minutes. You can do them in the morning or afternoon, but not right after a meal. Even though we are saluting the sun, it is not a good idea to do your yoga practice in direct sunlight, so try to find a warm, quiet spot with even lighting.

week 1 • mountain pose

Let the strength
of your back give
you confidence.

Let the softness of your
front invite you to be open
to whatever arises.

Mountain pose teaches us how to balance on two feet, find length in the spine, and feel freedom in our breath. As we gaze straight ahead, we can meet the world with open eyes and an open heart. Just like a mountain, in this pose we extend up toward heaven and down to earth at the same time. Try to find this connection to heaven and earth in every pose.

As the sun shines on us and our world, just like plants, we begin a process of unfolding. What is your experience of that process? Comfortable, challenging, scary, fun?

Look up and see your palms meeting.

Press your palms together
by using your arm muscles.

As you reach your arms up,
reach your feet down, so that
your whole body lengthens
in two directions.

Mountain pose with arms overhead opens the shoulders and the upper back area and strengthens the heart and lungs. It also increases lung capacity.

Are you breathing? Do you tend to hold your breath? What makes you sigh?

week 3 • standing forward bend

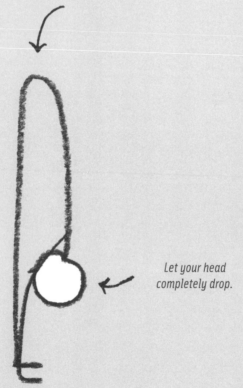

Let your upper body be like a
waterfall pouring out of your strong legs.

Let your head
completely drop.

Standing forward bend lengthens the entire back of the body, including the
hamstrings and the lower back. It also releases and lengthens the spine and neck.

How was the first sun salute of the day different from the last? From yesterday's? How does that difference relate to the weather, your mood, what you ate for breakfast, how you slept?

week 4 • lunge, right leg back

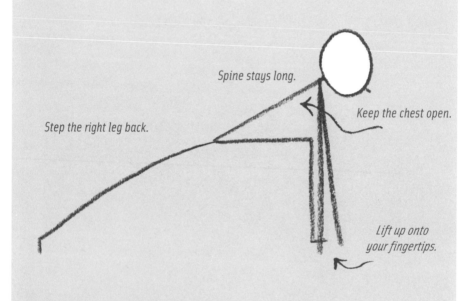

Spine stays long.

Keep the chest open.

Step the right leg back.

Lift up onto
your fingertips.

Lunge, right leg back creates strength in the legs and increases mobility in the hips.

What is the texture of your mind: speedy or sluggish?
How does this texture change throughout your practice?

week 5 • downward dog

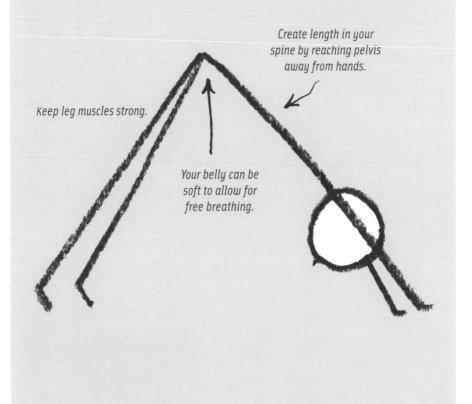

Create length in your spine by reaching pelvis away from hands.

Keep leg muscles strong.

Your belly can be soft to allow for free breathing.

Downward dog creates strength in the arms and legs and flexibility in the shoulders and hips.

Do you prefer one experience of the sun salute over another? Why? Can you taste all your experiences of the sun salute without judging them or trying to "improve" them?

week 6 • plank pose

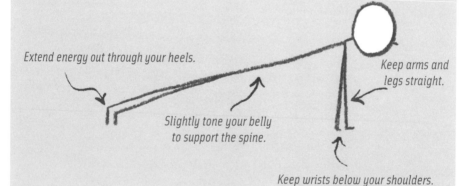

Extend energy out through your heels.

Slightly tone your belly
to support the spine.

Keep arms and
legs straight.

Keep wrists below your shoulders.

Plank pose creates strength in the arms, legs, and abdominal muscles.

Has your sun salute practice affected your daily life in any way?

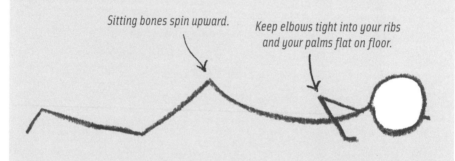

Sitting bones spin upward.

Keep elbows tight into your ribs
and your palms flat on floor.

Knees, chest, chin opens the hips, chest, and the upper and middle back.

Where does your body feel bright? Where do you feel dull?

week 8 • baby cobra

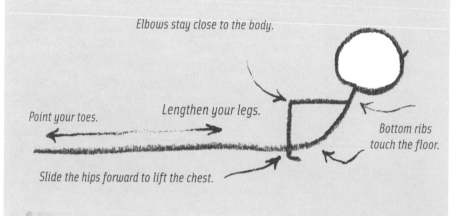

Elbows stay close to the body.

Lengthen your legs.

Point your toes.

Bottom ribs touch the floor.

Slide the hips forward to lift the chest.

Baby cobra tones the spine and strengthens the back of the body, including legs and buttocks.

What is the same about the sun salute every day?
What is the same about you every day?

week 9 • downward dog

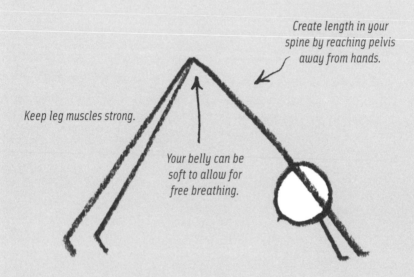

Create length in your spine by reaching pelvis away from hands.

Keep leg muscles strong.

Your belly can be soft to allow for free breathing.

Downward dog creates strength in the legs and increases mobility in the hips.

How does the heat of the sun salute affect your body?

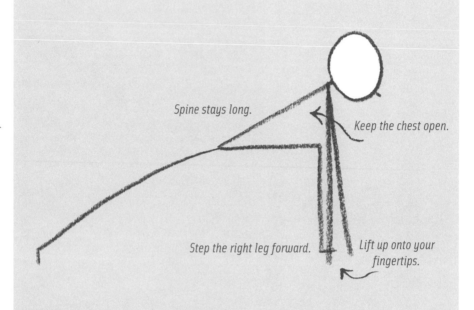

Spine stays long.

Keep the chest open.

Step the right leg forward.

Lift up onto your fingertips.

Lunge, right leg forward creates strength in the legs and increases mobility in the hips; it also tones abdominal muscles and helps you to develop coordination.

Are you getting looser or tighter? Maybe both at the same time?
In your mind or your body? Maybe both at the same time?

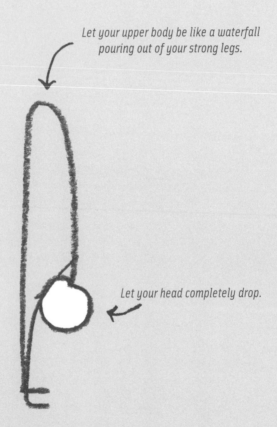

Let your upper body be like a waterfall
pouring out of your strong legs.

Let your head completely drop.

Standing forward bend *lengthens the entire back of the body, including your hamstrings and your lower back. It also releases and lengthens the spine and neck.*

Have your friends or family noticed any changes in you mentally, emotionally, or physically? What are they?

week 12 • mountain pose with arms overhead

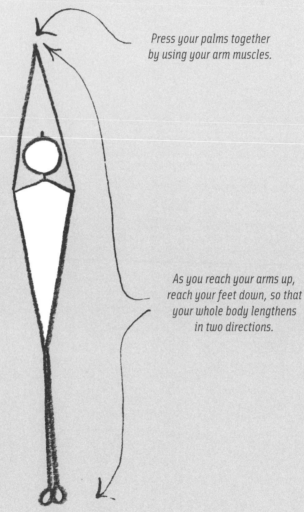

Look up and see your palms meeting.

Press your palms together by using your arm muscles.

As you reach your arms up, reach your feet down, so that your whole body lengthens in two directions.

Mountain pose with arms overhead opens the shoulders and upper back area and strengthens your heart and lungs. This pose also increases your lung capacity.

What's it like to do your yoga practice when you don't feel like it?

week 13 • mountain pose

Reach up to heaven with
the crown of your head.

Feel your feet reaching
down into the earth.

Mountain pose teaches us how to balance on two feet and find length in the spine and freedom in the breath. As we gaze straight ahead, we can meet the world with open eyes and open heart. Just like a mountain, in this pose we extend up toward heaven and down to earth at the same time. Try to find this connection to heaven and earth in every pose.

Have you experienced any benefits from doing the sun salute? What are they?

Summer: GETTING STRONG AND FREE
Standing Poses and Hip Openers

One of my favorite childhood memories is going outside on summer nights to play with my friends after dinner. The screen door swung wide open as I raced out into the soft warmth of the northwest summer evening to marvel at the fireflies, turn somersaults in the grass, and watch as the light slowly dimmed in the safety of my own front yard.

Summer is still the season when most of us love to go outside and play: swimming, jogging on the beach, playing volleyball, Rollerblading, biking, hiking. But let's face it, if you're not feeling strong, fit, and energetic, playing isn't as fun as it was when you were a kid.

The main impediments to moving through space are physical weakness, low energy, and tightness in the hip area. We will tackle these issues with a summertime *vinyasa* that cultivates stamina through standing poses, flexibility through hip openers, and strength and focus through balancing poses.

As this season of full blossoming vibrates throughout your body, you may begin to notice that your confidence grows as well. The outward movement of our bodies is naturally reflected in a flowering of our hearts and minds, which can even radiate out to our relationships with other people and with the whole world.

Summer

4 wide standing forward bend

5 tree pose

8 downward dog

9 cobbler's pose

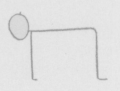

12 seated twist

13 table top

① warrior one   ② warrior two   ③ extended side angle

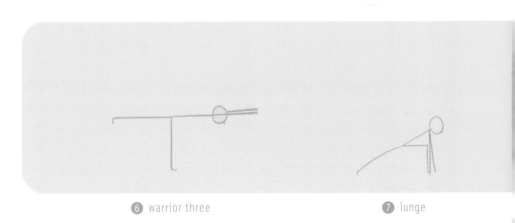

⑥ warrior three   ⑦ lunge

⑩ head to knee pose   ⑪ boat pose

Standing Poses and Hip Openers

This *vinyasa* is designed to be done one pose after another, but if you feel that you need to work up to doing that, it's no problem. You can work on each pose slowly and one by one, eventually connect them in short sequences.

Do the standing pose sequence, poses 1 to 6, first with the right leg forward, then the left leg, before continuing with the rest of the series. Do the last twist in both directions.

Never get aggressive with hip openers. Many of us have a tendency to push our knees apart or to pull with our arms in these poses, but doing that is counterproductive. Come into the position, deepen your breathing, and watch how your body unfolds, slowly but surely, over time.

I recommend that you do the sun salute series at least two times before you begin this sequence.

week 1 • warrior one

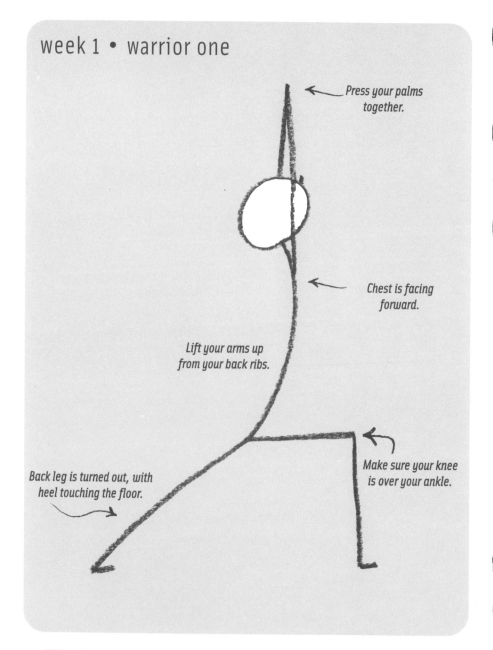

Press your palms together.

Chest is facing forward.

Lift your arms up from your back ribs.

Make sure your knee is over your ankle.

Back leg is turned out, with heel touching the floor.

Warrior one strengthens the arms and legs and relieves stiffness in the shoulders and back.

Standing poses help you to develop strength, but it often takes time to gain that strength. How can this sequence help you cultivate patience as well as strength?

week 2 • warrior two

Make space between your shoulder blades.

Keep your spine vertical.

Use your inner thigh muscles to support your back leg.

Warrior two strengthens the arms and legs and opens the hips.

*Are you breathing? How does your breath change
in balancing poses, seated poses, standing poses?*

Feel one long line of energy from heel all the way through fingertips.

Extended side angle strengthens the arms and legs, opens the hips, and stretches the waist, shoulders, and muscles around the rib cage.

How can you stay relaxed within the effort of these asanas?

week 4 • wide-standing forward bend

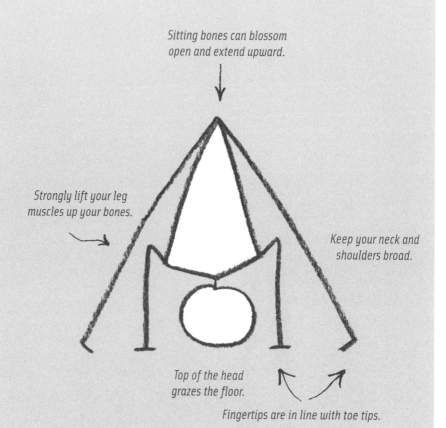

Sitting bones can blossom
open and extend upward.

Strongly lift your leg
muscles up your bones.

Keep your neck and
shoulders broad.

Top of the head
grazes the floor.

Fingertips are in line with toe tips.

Wide-standing forward bend strengthens the legs, opens the hips, and lengthens the spine.

Which part of your body gets tired first?
What happens first—tired body or bored mind?

week 5 • tree pose

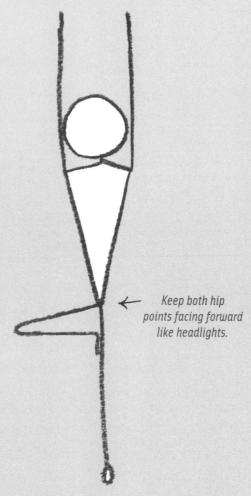

← *Keep both hip points facing forward like headlights.*

Can you feel yourself rooting and rising at the same time?

Tree pose *develops concentration and a sense of equanimity.*

What has your experience of this summertime vinyasa been so far?

week 6 • warrior three

Keep the back of your neck long by looking down.

Reach out through every finger.

Lift belly up to support your spine.

Flex your foot and strongly
reach back so your foot and
whole leg feel like someone
is pulling your sock off.

Warrior three teaches balance and courage and helps develop evenness of extension.

What are your favorite memories of summertime?

week 7 • lunge

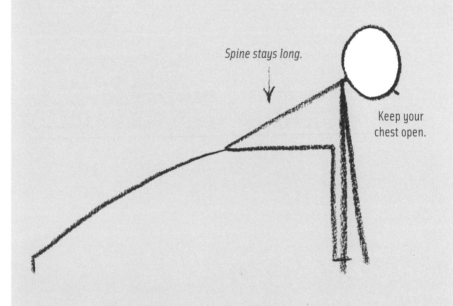

Spine stays long.

Keep your
chest open.

Lunge creates strength in the legs and increases mobility in the hips; it also tones abdominal muscles and helps you to develop coordination.

What is the best time of day for you to practice yoga in the summer?

week 8 • downward dog

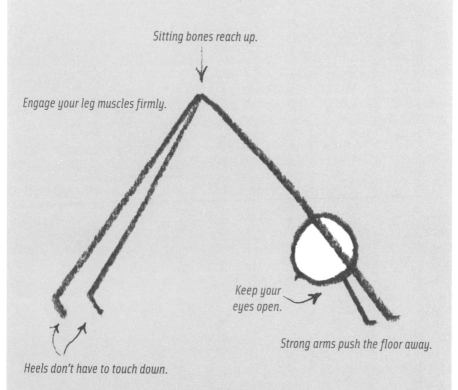

Sitting bones reach up.

Engage your leg muscles firmly.

Keep your eyes open.

Strong arms push the floor away.

Heels don't have to touch down.

Downward dog *creates strength in the legs and increases mobility in the hips.*

Has your yoga practice affected your other physical activities in any way?

If your pelvis tucks under and your back slumps, sit on one or two cushions.

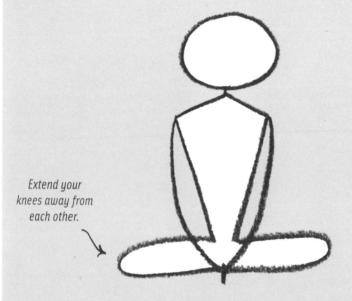

Extend your knees away from each other.

Press your heels together and hold onto your ankles.

Cobbler's pose *increases blood flow to the pelvic region, which is beneficial to the urinary tract and to prostate, menstrual, and menopausal health.*

How does the heat of the day affect your energy, body, and mind?

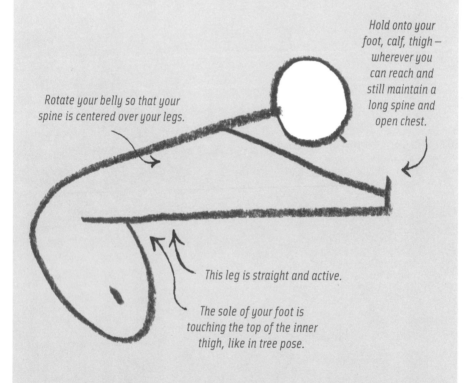

Rotate your belly so that your spine is centered over your legs.

Hold onto your foot, calf, thigh — wherever you can reach and still maintain a long spine and open chest.

This leg is straight and active.

The sole of your foot is touching the top of the inner thigh, like in tree pose.

Head to knee pose *increases flexibility in the hamstrings, hips, and lumbar area.*

Is your yoga practice the fun part of the day or something you do because it's good for you? Can it be a little bit of both?

week 11 • boat pose

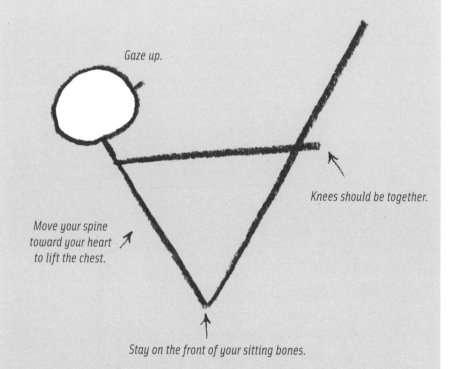

Gaze up.

Move your spine
toward your heart
to lift the chest.

Knees should be together.

Stay on the front of your sitting bones.

Boat pose *strengthens the back and the abdominals.*

Have you noticed any relationship between your yoga practice and how you sleep? How you eat?

week 12 • seated twist

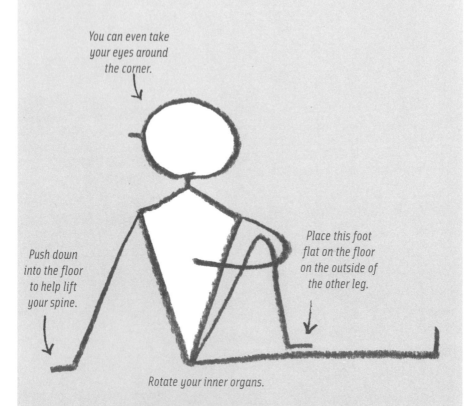

You can even take your eyes around the corner.

Push down into the floor to help lift your spine.

Place this foot flat on the floor on the outside of the other leg.

Rotate your inner organs.

Seated twist *tones the waist and the abdominal organs, relieves headaches, and increases flexibility in the hips and lower back.*

How is the balance of your upper body and lower body shifting?

week 13 • tabletop

You can let your head drop,
be natural, or look forward.
Make it comfortable for you.

Let your belly drop.

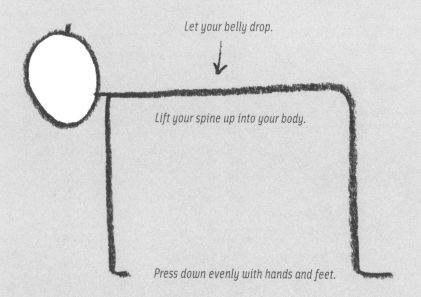

Lift your spine up into your body.

Press down evenly with hands and feet.

Tabletop strengthens the wrists, arms, hamstrings, and buttocks and opens the chest and shoulders.

Note which poses are your favorites and which are your least favorites. Watch how these preferences change over time.

Autumn: OPENING OUR HEARTS AND CLEANING HOUSE
Backbends and Twists

The crisp, exhilarating autumn air holds a soulful mix of falling leaves, gratitude, crackling bonfires, and a sense of completion. As the trees begin to let go of their leaves, more and more space opens up, and we can literally see farther than we could before. This outward opening merges with the melancholy of the season, creating a sense of fullness that manifests in the richness of the season, family, and holidays of homecoming and thanksgiving.

Autumn is the perfect season to practice backbends, the heart-opening poses of yoga. Backbends increase flexibility in the spine, strengthen the back muscles, improve digestion, and open the chest and lungs. Backbends are invigorating and can even lift us out of depression, so as daylight time grows shorter, they can be a way to keep your spirits up. Backbends are also good for developing courage. Turning yourself upside down and inside out takes a certain amount of pluck, and for most of us, it's quite a challenge. The more that we can practice facing our fears, the more we can cultivate fearlessness, which over time translates into a grounded confidence as we move through the day.

This autumn yoga sequence also includes several twists that not only rebalance the spine after backbending but also are like cleaning house, because they wring out the toxins stored in our abdominal organs. When you twist, your organs get squeezed and when you untwist they are soaked in the freshly oxygenated blood that rushes back in. This squeeze-and-soak action refreshes and nourishes our body, just as this time of year does the same for our hearts.

Autumn

④ lunge and psoas stretch

⑤ pigeon

⑧ locust

⑨ bow

⑫ rotated seated straddle

⑬ seated forward bend

① cow's head arms

② seated spinal twist

③ downward dog split / hip opener

⑥ pigeon with quadricep stretch

⑦ cobra

⑩ half-wheel

⑪ supine twist

Backbends and Twists

Do poses 1 to 6 to each side before continuing the rest of the sequence. Make sure you do the supine twist and the rotated seated straddle to both sides.

Because backbends can be energizing, I don't recommend doing them before bed. Take your time with these poses. Let your breath move into the tight places, and as if you were getting a massage, slowly release those areas over time.

Only twist as far as feels comfortable to you. Wait there and watch how your twist naturally deepens with your exhale.

week 1 • cow's head arms

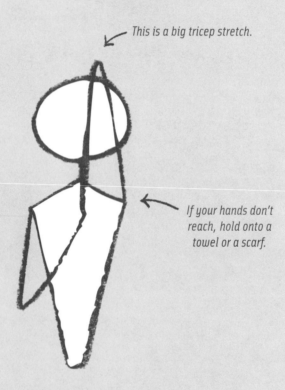

This is a big tricep stretch.

If your hands don't reach, hold onto a towel or a scarf.

Cow's head arms opens the shoulder joints and stretches the triceps.

*What is the relationship between your yoga practice
and your physical energy this autumn?*

week 2 • seated spinal twist

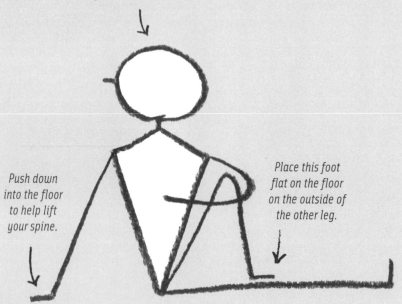

You can even take your
eyes around the corner.

Push down
into the floor
to help lift
your spine.

Place this foot
flat on the floor
on the outside of
the other leg.

Rotate your inner organs.

Seated spinal twist *relieves headaches, strengthens the back and neck muscles, opens the shoulders, and tones abdominal organs.*

Is it easier to twist to the left or the right?
Do you know why? Does it vary?

week 3 • downward dog split / hip opener

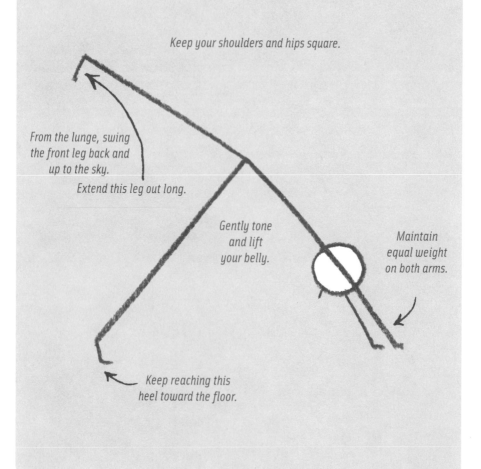

Keep your shoulders and hips square.

From the lunge, swing the front leg back and up to the sky.

Extend this leg out long.

Gently tone and lift your belly.

Maintain equal weight on both arms.

Keep reaching this heel toward the floor.

Downward dog split / hip opener lengthens the hamstring on one leg while opening the front of the other hip and thigh.

What are your memories of this time of year?

week 4 • lunge and psoas stretch

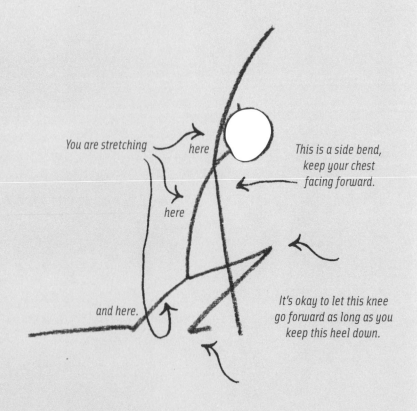

You are stretching *here*

here

and here.

This is a side bend, keep your chest facing forward.

It's okay to let this knee go forward as long as you keep this heel down.

Lunge and psoas stretch stretches the psoas muscle and opens the shoulder area.

Backbends require opening in the shoulders and hips.
What is your experience of that in this backbending preparation?

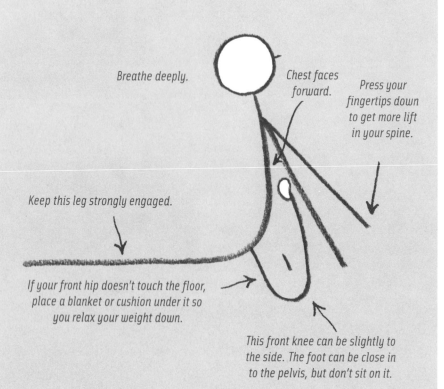

Breathe deeply.

Chest faces forward.

Press your fingertips down to get more lift in your spine.

Keep this leg strongly engaged.

If your front hip doesn't touch the floor, place a blanket or cushion under it so you relax your weight down.

This front knee can be slightly to the side. The foot can be close in to the pelvis, but don't sit on it.

Pigeon opens the hips and hamstrings and tones the spine.

Are you breathing? How does your breathing help you in backbending?

week 6 • pigeon with quad stretch

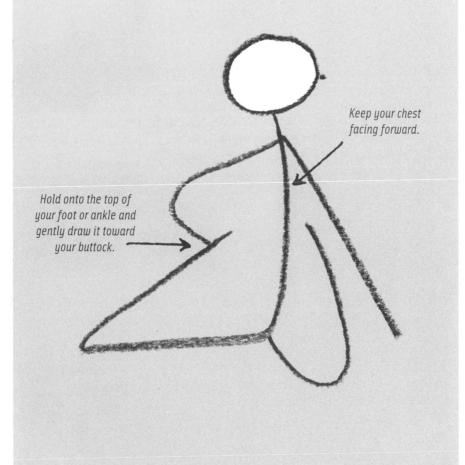

Keep your chest facing forward.

Hold onto the top of your foot or ankle and gently draw it toward your buttock.

Pigeon with quad stretch opens the hips and hamstrings, tones the spine, and lengthens the quadricep muscles on the front of the back thigh.

Can you feel a connection to your heart in this pose?
Physically, emotionally?

week 7 • cobra

Keep your neck long and open.

This is a nice chest opener.

You can do this with straight arms, or you can do baby cobra, or somewhere in between—arms bent a little bit is okay.

Push down into the floor.

Keep your legs strong and active.

Cobra rejuvenates the spine, opens the chest, and expands lung capacity.

Do you like backbending? Why? Why not?
How does that feeling change from day to day?

Think of touching the wall behind you with your toes.

Breathe with the back of the neck.

Lift from the sternum and heart.

Locust strengthens the back muscles and relieves back pain.

Can you recognize the shapes of these poses in nature? Where?

week 9 • bow

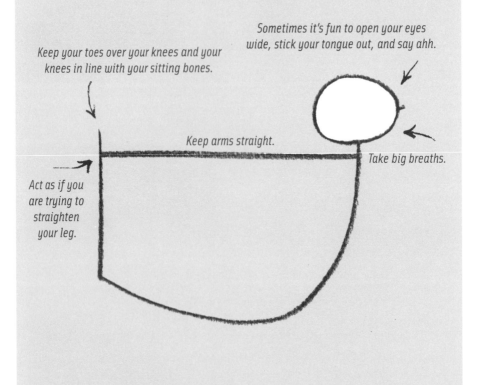

Keep your toes over your knees and your knees in line with your sitting bones.

Sometimes it's fun to open your eyes wide, stick your tongue out, and say ahh.

Keep arms straight.

Take big breaths.

Act as if you are trying to straighten your leg.

Bow opens the chest, tones the abdominal organs, and creates flexibility in the spine.

Can you use your breath to open your heart more?

week 10 • half-wheel

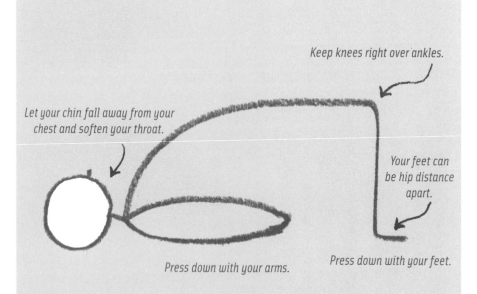

Keep knees right over ankles.

Let your chin fall away from your chest and soften your throat.

Your feet can be hip distance apart.

Press down with your arms.

Press down with your feet.

Half-wheel opens the chest, strengthens the arms and legs, and generates vitality and energy.

Do you feel energized by doing backbends?
Try doing them before an important meeting and see what happens.

week 11 • supine twist

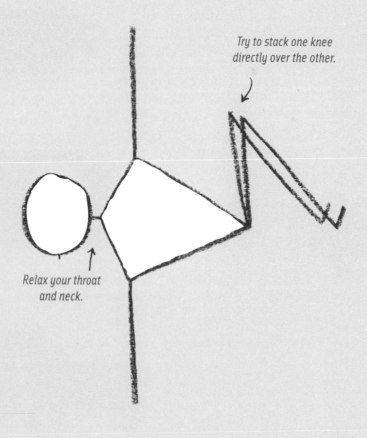

Try to stack one knee directly over the other.

Relax your throat and neck.

Supine twist trims the waist, energizes the abdominal organs, and relieves tightness in the lower back and hips.

How has your yoga practice affected your other physical activities?

week 12 • rotated seated straddle

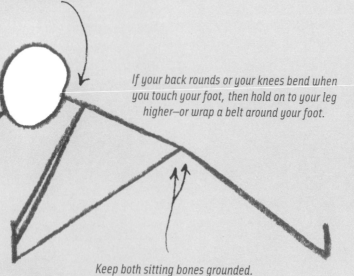

Rotate your chest to face your leg in a slight twist.

If your back rounds or your knees bend when you touch your foot, then hold on to your leg higher—or wrap a belt around your foot.

Keep both sitting bones grounded.

Rotated seated straddle *massages inner organs and the lumbar area, stretches the hamstrings, and improves reproductive and pelvic health by increasing circulation to the area.*

How does your yoga practice change when you do it faster or slower?

week 13 • seated forward bend

Once again, hold on wherever you can reach and still keep your spine straight. Use a belt if you need to. Reach through your sternum, keeping the spine long as you fold over your legs.

Make sure your chest is open and your breath is free. You never want your pose to inhibit your heart and lung activity.

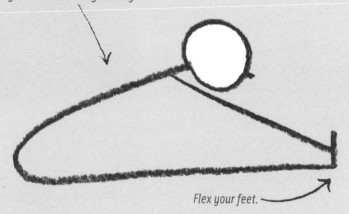

Flex your feet.

Seated forward bend lengthens the entire back of the body, including the legs, and massages the heart and abdominal organs.

What does it feel like to be you right now?

Winter: GOING INSIDE
Forward Bends and Restorative Yoga

Winter powerfully reminds us of the importance of resting. We only need to observe our natural environment—barren trees and flower beds, cold temperatures, gray skies—to understand that our own organic rhythm at this time of year reflects this downcycling of activity. It is the perfect time to go inside; not just inside our physical shelters, but inside ourselves.

Much of our yoga practice is about putting our bodies into specific shapes, staying there mindfully, and experiencing benefits of strength, flexibility, and physical well-being. But our yoga practice is not just about doing; it is also about being.

In yoga, the opposite of active is not passive, but receptive. For many of us, learning to be quiet, open, and receptive to whatever arises is one of the most difficult challenges in our lives. In our wintertime yoga series we enter this inner journey through the calming effect of forward bends and the rejuvenating positions of restorative poses.

Perhaps the dark and quiet hours of winter will become the best time for growth—inward growth that deepens our understanding of ourselves so that we can be whole and rested for the awakening that spring holds.

Winter

4 extended child's pose

5 star pose

8 rotated head-to-knee pose

9 supine twist

12 reclining twist

13 supported child's pose

1 standing forward bend   **2** downward dog   **3** cow/cat pose

6 seated straddle forward bend   **7** seated forward bend

10 supported bound-angle pose   **11** legs-up-the wall pose

Forward Bends and Restorative Yoga

Don't pull on your legs during forward bends. This will only generate craving for your experience to be different than it is right now.

Make sure that your body is completely supported in the restorative poses so you can fully relax.

Try to stay in each restorative pose for five to ten minutes, but feel free to stay longer if you like.

week 1 • standing forward bend

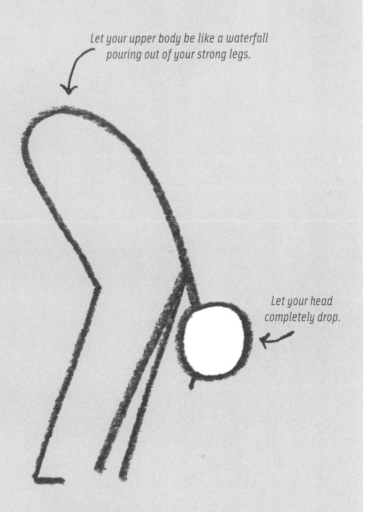

Let your upper body be like a waterfall pouring out of your strong legs.

Let your head completely drop.

Standing forward bend lengthens the entire back of the body, including the hamstrings and the lower back. It also releases and lengthens the spine and neck.

What does it feel like to practice yoga in the winter?
What does it feel like to generate your own heat through yoga asanas?

week 2 • downward dog

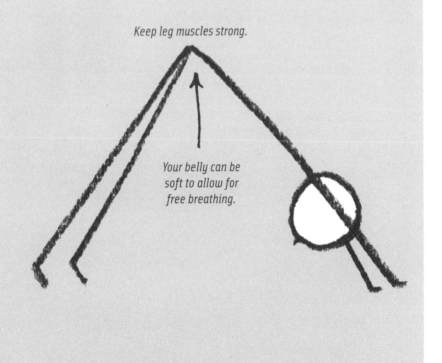

Keep leg muscles strong.

Your belly can be soft to allow for free breathing.

Downward dog creates strength in the legs and increases mobility in the hips.

Are you breathing? How does your breath change in forward bends, in downward dog, and in restorative postures?

week 3 • cow / cat pose

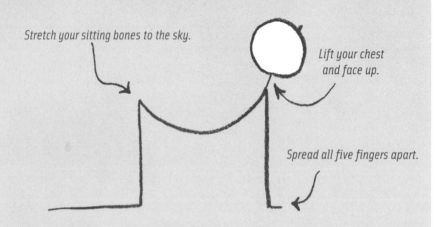

Stretch your sitting bones to the sky.

Lift your chest and face up.

Spread all five fingers apart.

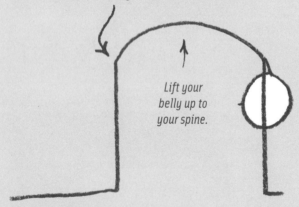

Tuck your tailbone and head under.

Lift your belly up to your spine.

Cow / cat pose increases flexibility in the spine.

Are you able to remain wakeful within the quiet
and relaxation of this winter yoga sequence?

week 4 • extended child's pose

Rest here, ahh...

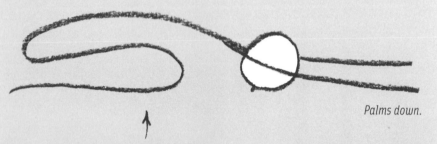

Palms down.

↑

*Keep your feet together and separate
your knees as wide apart as you can.*

Extended child's pose *opens the hips, shoulders, and triceps.*

What is it like to do the other seasons' sequences during the winter?

week 5 • star pose

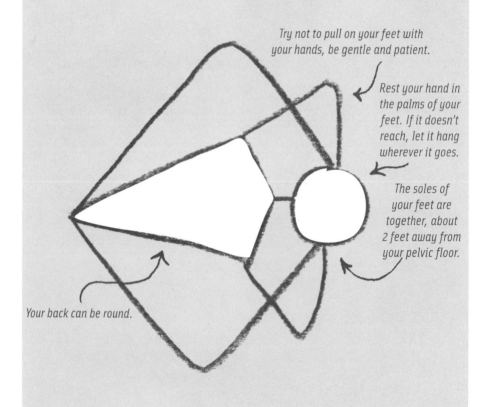

Try not to pull on your feet with your hands, be gentle and patient.

Rest your hand in the palms of your feet. If it doesn't reach, let it hang wherever it goes.

The soles of your feet are together, about 2 feet away from your pelvic floor.

Your back can be round.

Star pose gently opens hips and lengthens the back, including the neck.

It is said that restorative yoga poses do you,
instead of you doing them. Is that your experience?

week 6 • seated straddle forward bend

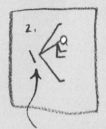

It takes quite a while for almost everybody to do this, so start here with your back straight, chest open, and fingertips on the floor slightly in front of you.

Use a blanket or cushion under your hips.

Eventually you may get your forearms down.

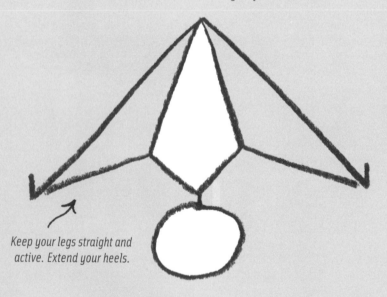

Keep your legs straight and active. Extend your heels.

Seated straddle forward bend stretches the hamstrings and improves reproductive and pelvic health by increasing circulation to the area.

Do you have any recurring thoughts during your yoga practice?
Are they different in some poses than in others,
for example, in standing poses versus restorative poses?

week 7 • seated forward bend

Make sure your chest is open
and your breath is free. You
never want your pose to inhibit
your heart and lung activity.

Once again, hold on wherever
you can reach and still keep
your spine straight. Use a belt
if you need to. Reach through
your sternum, keeping the
spine long as you fold over
your legs.

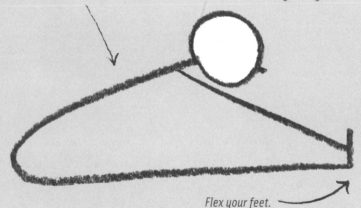

Flex your feet.

Seated forward bend lengthens the entire back of the body, including the legs,
and massages the heart and abdominal organs.

How is your yoga practice different during the week and on weekends?

week 8 • rotated head-to-knee pose

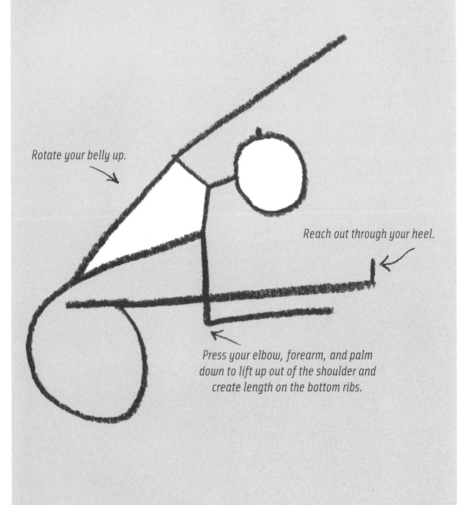

Rotate your belly up.

Reach out through your heel.

Press your elbow, forearm, and palm down to lift up out of the shoulder and create length on the bottom ribs.

Rotated head-to-knee pose *aids digestion and relieves backaches.*

How are you affected by your environment?
The weather? Your family? How does yoga relate to that?

week 9 • supine twist

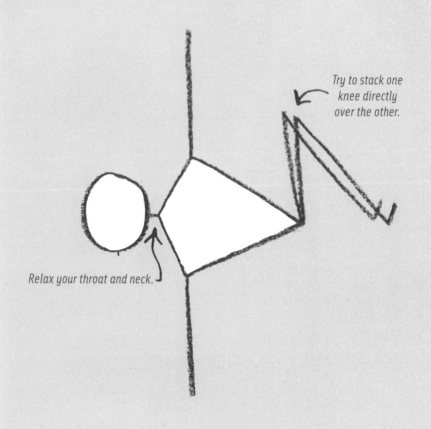

Try to stack one knee directly over the other.

Relax your throat and neck.

Supine twist *trims the waist, energizes the abdominal organs, and relieves tightness in the lower back and hips.*

Do you feel more connected to yourself through your yoga practice?

week 10 • supported bound-angle pose

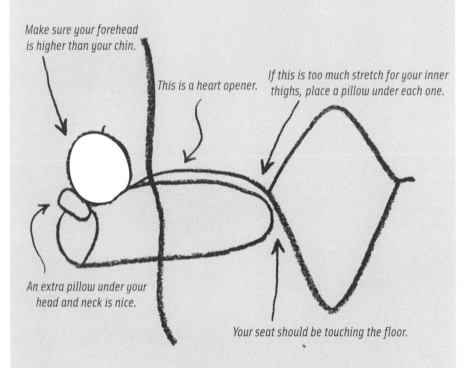

Make sure your forehead is higher than your chin.

This is a heart opener.

If this is too much stretch for your inner thighs, place a pillow under each one.

An extra pillow under your head and neck is nice.

Your seat should be touching the floor.

Supported bound-angle pose *opens the chest, abdominal area, and pelvis. This pose is good for prostate, menopausal, or menstrual issues.*

What benefits—physical, mental, emotional, spiritual—have you gotten from practicing yoga?

week 11 • legs-up-the-wall pose

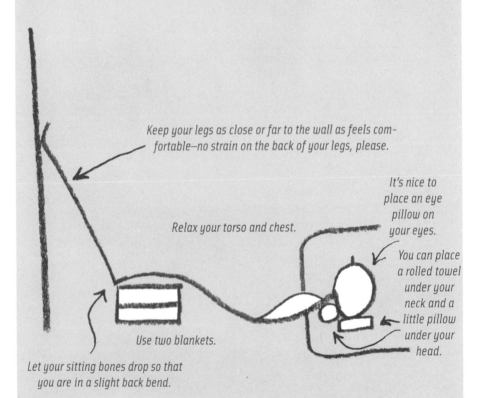

Keep your legs as close or far to the wall as feels comfortable—no strain on the back of your legs, please.

Relax your torso and chest.

It's nice to place an eye pillow on your eyes.

You can place a rolled towel under your neck and a little pillow under your head.

Use two blankets.

Let your sitting bones drop so that you are in a slight back bend.

Legs-up-the-wall pose *reverses fluid and swelling in the legs, refreshes the heart and lungs, and quiets the mind.*

Do you find it difficult to make time for yourself and your yoga practice?

week 12 • reclining twist

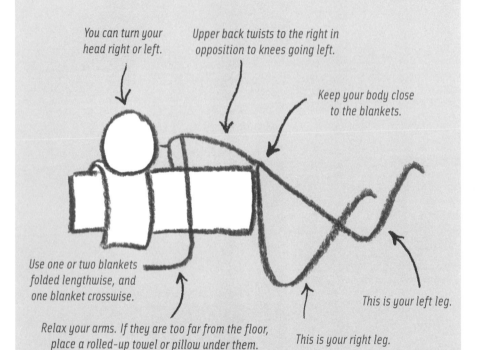

You can turn your head right or left.

Upper back twists to the right in opposition to knees going left.

Keep your body close to the blankets.

Use one or two blankets folded lengthwise, and one blanket crosswise.

Relax your arms. If they are too far from the floor, place a rolled-up towel or pillow under them.

This is your left leg.

This is your right leg.

Reclining twist *stretches the muscles of the side and back, and enhances deep breathing.*

Do you ever do your yoga practice with another person? What is that like?

week 13 • supported child's pose

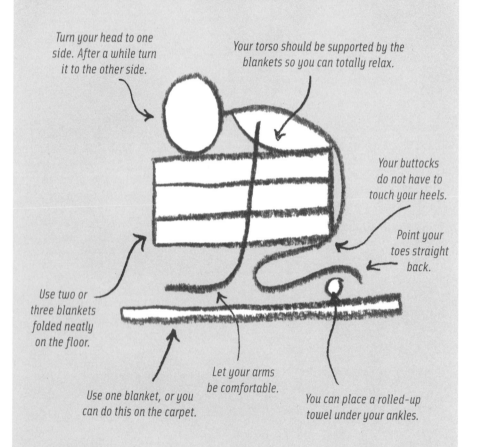

Turn your head to one side. After a while turn it to the other side.

Your torso should be supported by the blankets so you can totally relax.

Your buttocks do not have to touch your heels.

Point your toes straight back.

Use two or three blankets folded neatly on the floor.

Let your arms be comfortable.

Use one blanket, or you can do this on the carpet.

You can place a rolled-up towel under your ankles.

Supported child's pose *gently stretches the lower back and quiets the mind.*

When your body is quiet, does your mind seem louder? Can you recognize that this is the same mind you had before you noticed it? Can you recognize that your loud mind and your quiet mind are both yours?

glossary

Asana: This word refers to the physical postures of hatha yoga practice. It means "seat" or the part of your body that is touching the ground. For example, with the word *sirsasana*, *sirsa* is "head," and *asana* means "seat" so it means put your head on the ground or headstand.

Breathing: Conscious manipulated breathing is an essential part of yoga and traditionally called *pranayama*. *Prana* means "life force" and can be found in air, water, earth, sunshine, and humans and animals. We can most easily experience it and control it through conscious manipulated breathing techniques. *Ayama* means "extension," so *pranayama* is a series of breathing exercises designed to lengthen life as well as to improve the quality of it. Yogis say that each person has a predetermined number of breaths for his or her life, so the theory is that if you can learn to lengthen each breath, you will live longer.

Hatha: This often translates as "forceful" and refers to the energy and effort that is involved in asana practice. We often think of yoga as relaxing, but it takes strength of mind as well as muscle to hold your body in an *asana* for more than two seconds. This effort is part of the path to discovering spaciousness. Hatha yoga teaches us that rather than being aggressive, willpower can mean being wakeful, focused, and on the dot. This balance is also implied in the word *hatha*. *Ha* means "sun," which yoga philosophy considers to have masculine qualities of activity, heat, outward energy, and light. *Tha* means "moon," which contains the feminine qualities of receptivity, coolness, turning inward, and darkness.

Mudra: A physical seal—such as placing the thumb and first finger together—which creates a specific energetic circuit that will create a certain experience. For example, placing your palms flat on your thighs is called the *mudra* of calm abiding. You may feel that turning your palms down is like gently putting a lid on your overstimulated nervous system.

If you are sleepy while meditating, it is recommended that you use the cosmic *mudra*, which is palms turned up, fingers of one hand on top of the other with your thumb tips lightly touching. This *mudra* should be held slightly above your lap, and if you start to fall asleep, your hands will drop and awaken you.

Some *asanas*, such as the shoulder stand, are also considered *mudras*.

Om: The sound of Om is created from four parts: A, U, M, and the silence after the sound. The silence is called the *turiya* and is said to include all the sounds of the universe. It can be felt as a vibration and reminds us that all the sounds we hear—our heartbeats, thunder, birds singing, even jackhammers—are all sound manifestations of the pulsation of the cosmos that moves through all of us all the time.

Prana: *Prana* is the life force or primordial energy that flows through all living beings. *Prana* can also be found in elements that create life, such as sunlight, water, and earth.

Savasana: This is one of the most important poses in yoga practice. It is translated as the corpse pose and is traditionally done at the end of every yoga class. It gives our bodies a chance to assimilate all the benefits of the more active poses, as well as a chance for our body temperature to cool down after vigorous practice. Although it seems that *savasana* is like taking a nap, it has the same dynamic as all yoga poses, which is a balance of wakefulness and relaxation. So although your body may be still, in *savasana* yogis are invited to watch their minds and remain alert, just as in meditation practice.

Shamatha: Traditional Tibetan Buddhist meditation technique that means "calm abiding" or "resting in peace." It is done with the eyes open, using the breath as a reference point for returning to and resting in the present moment. This method of one-pointed concentration leads to an increased ability to concentrate and is the ground for yoga practice and more advanced meditation techniques.

In walking meditation, *shamatha* is merged with *vipassana*, or a lifting of the eyes during which the meditator begins to experience a larger awareness of the environment in her consciousness.

Vinyasa: This refers to a flowing form of yoga in which *asanas* are strung together like beads on a necklace, and the string that connects them is the breath. It can be done slowly and spaciously or faster, giving each asana only one breath. This form generates heat, cultivates coordination and gracefulness, and reminds us that the transitions are just as important as the poses.

Yoga: Yoga is a state of being, a feeling of union with all that is. It is also a series of practices that include codes of conduct, physical exercises, breathing exercises, and meditation.

resources

Books and Journals

Chödron, Pema. *The Wisdom of No Escape and the Path of Loving Kindness*. Boston: Shambhala, 1991.

Iyengar, B.K.S. *Light on Yoga*. New York: Schocken Books, 1966.

Lee, Cyndi. *OM Yoga: A Guide to Daily Practice*. San Francisco: Chronicle Books, 2002.

Lassiter, Judith. *Relax and Renew*. Berkeley, CA: Rodmell Press, 1995.

Schiffmann, Erich. *Yoga: The Spirit and Practice of Moving into Stillness*. New York: Simon & Schuster, 1996.

Yoga Journal. 2054 University Avenue, Suite 600, Berkeley, CA, 94704; (510) 841-9200; www.yogajournal.com.

Instructional Products

OM Yoga in a Box, Basic Level, For Couples, and Intermediate Level. Everything you need for a meaningful practice at home instructional CD, music CD, flashcards, incense, candle, yoga belt for stretching:
Lee, Cyndi. OM Yoga in a Box Basic Level. Cambridge, MA; Padma Projects, 1999.
——. OM Yoga in a Box For Couples. Cambridge, MA: Padma Projects, 2000.
——. OM Yoga in a Box Intermediate Level. Cambridge, MA: Padma Projects, 2001.

Yee, Rodney. (Videos - various) Berkeley, CA: Healing Arts
Publishing, 1996.

Information about Yoga Retreats

Retreats with Cyndi Lee: www.omyoga.com

Omega Institute: Retreat center in upstate New York and retreats
worldwide
Omega Institute for Holistic Studies
150 Lake Drive
Rhinebeck, NY 12752
(845) 266-4444
www.eomega.org

Esalen—Retreats in Northern California
www.esalen.org

For listings of yoga centers in your area, contact
Yoga Journal Resource Guide at www.yogajournal.com.